TIP$ FOR BETTER

TIP$

MENU FOR SUCCE$$

Increase Your Gratuities
A Server's Guide To:

TIP$ FOR BETTER

TIP$

MENU FOR SUCCE$$

An easy-to-read guide to help promote the
EDGE-ucation that will create
a Win-Win environment for you and the entire
establishment.

What are you waiting for?

David S. Capeloto

A Special Thanks

To all the owners, managers, and servers I had the privilege to work with for over twenty-five years, and most of all learn from. To my family whose unconditional love and support never wavered. And a special thank you to my good friends Michael and Sandra who motivate me, keep me focused, and moving forward. And to my most influential mentors Joe Esposito and Mario Vincitorio, from whom I learned so much. I can't thank you both enough. Thank you!

"Common Sense

Is Not

So Common"

~Voltaire

Foreword

I am humbled to be considered a mentor by my dear friend David Capeloto, the author of this essential and highly informative book.

David worked as a server for seven years in the second of my three fine dining restaurants I've owned in the past thirty-five years. He was easily the most professional, successful, and most requested, of any server I've employed over the years.

Everyone knows the crucial importance of excellent service in the restaurant industry, but David turned taking care of customers into a fine art. More importantly, the knowledge, techniques, and common sense he employed are now available to everyone in this business.

While this book is written for servers, every restaurant owner and manager will benefit from his knowledge and expertise, and so will the bottom line!!

God speed to you, David, and to all your readers.

Mario V. Restaurant Owner, Tempe, AZ.

Introduction

Your mission, should you decide to accept it, is to increase the check's bottom line. This book will not self-destruct in five seconds, enabling you to review its powerful contents at any time. Making more money is, or at least should be, the goal of every server in the food and beverage industry. The bigger the bottom line, the bigger the TIP. The owners make more money. The servers make more money. The server assistants make more money. The bartenders make more money. This is a win-win situation for everyone. This is a winning program that will make it happen. Guaranteed.

Tip\$ For Better Tip\$—Menu For Success is an accumulation of knowledge both practiced as well as learned from the many servers, managers, and owners I had the privilege to work with over the years. Years of research, observation, and asking many questions revealed there was a noticeable difference among the best and most successful servers. What is the difference? I'm glad you asked.

You are soon to discover the essentials that will guarantee you an increase in the bottom line.

Tip\$ For Better Tip\$—Menu For Success is designed to be an easy-to-read guide to help promote the ***EDGE*-ucation** that will create a win-win environment for the entire establishment. Applying the principles you will learn from this book will greatly improve your skills and abilities as a professional server. Your service and confidence levels soar immediately.

Contents

*"We are what we repeatedly do.
Excellence then, is not an act,
but habit."*

~Aristotle

Tip$ For Better Tip$

Menu For Success

Do you want to make more money? **Tip$ For Better Tip$—Menu For Success** will make that happen for you—and literally overnight. Many servers I have worked with over the years have asked me how I do so well with tips. A number of my answers seemed easy to me, but I realized that not everyone had the benefit of my past experience. They say if people hear something, they will retain a certain portion of what they hear. On the other hand, if they read something, they retain a much larger percentage. This is why I have put into writing ideas on not only what works for me, but for many others as well. It's time for you to start making the money you deserve. Your guests want, deserve, and expect outstanding service. **Give it to them!!**

Can you believe that the Number One Complaint

about restaurants

(the ultimate service industry)

is

Poor Service

Wait staff training

is the key to

the restaurant's success!!!

Not sure if you should invest in training

for your staff? Not sure if you should

invest in yourself?

Some startling facts regarding the reasons businesses lose customers.

Let's start with some basic data. According to a study conducted by a Washington D.C. consulting firm, it was found that:

- More than 90 percent of dissatisfied customers will not return to your establishment again.

- For every unhappy customer, there are nine or more people who will tell others about their poor experience.

- As with anything else, people are 11 times more likely to relate their bad experiences than the good ones.

- Of those unhappy customers, 13 percent will reach 20 people or more with their tales of discontent.

The recipe for the perfect server includes many diverse ingredients and is not limited to knowledge, trust, personality, agility, grace, teamwork, or patience.

Recent studies indicate why customers may not return to your restaurant:

- 68 percent have encountered indifferent attitudes.

- 19 percent switch to competitors.

- 9 percent change lifestyle(e.g., diet).

- 4 percent move or are no longer with us.

Confidence – not arrogance

Service Begins
and Ends
With The Server

A survey conducted by the National Restaurant Association shows what guests expect from servers.

Guests expect you to:

- Smile.

- Put them at ease.

- Ask whether they want additional items.

- Say how long before the order will be served.

- Be knowledgeable about the menu and how food is prepared.

Now the bad news: the top 10 "pet peeves" of restaurant customers:

- Slow service

- Bad tasting food

- High prices

- Cold food

- Poor service

- Children

- Surly server

- Too much noise

- Smokers

- Lack of cleanliness

*The wait staff is the face
of the restaurant.
They are the representatives,
your best source of advertising.*

Success begins and ends with great service.

Ahead are a variety of categories of utmost importance.

Read and practice these,

and I promise you your sales

will increase and so will your tips. That's the bottom line.

More money!

More Money!!

More Money!!!

More money!!!!

Tip 1

Smile/Personality

A genuine smile, along with a great personality, can set the tone for the entire dining experience. It starts the moment the guests enter the restaurant and with the first hello from the host/ess. This is also where the first impression of your restaurant is formed. This is entirely in the hands of the wait staff. You can't train someone to have a personality. However, you can train people with a great personality to be great at what they do. Do you, the moment you enter the restaurant, feel welcome? A genuine smile is very contagious and can certainly cheer up someone who may not be having the best of days. Keep on that happy face! Happy customers will tip more with a smile of their own.

Tip 2

Attitude

I cannot stress enough how important it is to have a good attitude. A good attitude is a noticeable thing. A bad attitude is even more noticeable. If you are having a bad day, leave it at home. Your guests are counting on a pleasant experience, and the server (in this case, you) is key. This can be very difficult at times, but your guests deserve you at your best. Guests do notice these things, just as you would. Stay positive and keep a good attitude.

Tip 3

Personal Preparation

A great server is always prepared. You should have your wine key, plenty of pens, and your station ready to go before opening. Be cleaned up, have the specials memorized along with any 86'd items, and your order pad/paper. Write orders down. Do not make any mistakes. Your side station should be well stocked, and of course a great attitude is your most valuable equipment of all. If you wait until you have a customer, you may find yourself scrambling for all the information and materials you need. Once you're behind, you may find it difficult to catch up. After all you wouldn't want your doctor or dentist to examine you with out the proper equipment. Be a pro and be prepared.

Tip 4

Hygiene and Grooming

Make sure you are clean and well groomed. The men should be clean-shaven and hair combed neatly. Beards/mustaches/goatees, if allowed, should also be neatly groomed. Women's hair, if long, should be tied back. Uniforms should be clean and wrinkle free. Avoid the wearing of colognes or perfumes while at work. People want to enjoy the fragrances of the restaurant, and if you are overpowering, it can take away from the overall ambience/smells of the restaurant and the taste of the food.

While on the floor, avoid playing with your hair, scratching your head or anywhere else. Biting your nails or scratching/picking your nose is definitely on the do not do list. This is certainly not very sanitary, and if a guest should notice, I'm sure they are hoping you will wash your hands before resuming service. In some cases the guest's will report to a manager what they have seen. Who needs that! It can be embarrassing as well, especially if it is your customer.

Tip 5

The 90% Rule

5% ———————— 90% ———————— 5%

No matter who you are, how good you are, how good the food was, how terrific everything was, there are 5% of your guests that just will not give you a good tip. Sometimes we refer to this as the dreaded verbal tip. On the other side of the scale there are people who will tip very well under almost any conditions, no matter what, to your pleasant surprise. Perhaps these people are restaurant or service-oriented people. Who knows? It's the 90% in the middle where you earn the majority of your money. We don't know where they may fall on the scale. Sometimes we have a tendency to assume how a guest may treat us, tip wise, and we end up totally wrong. Never pre-judge. Treat everyone like a V.I.P and don't take any chances. Be a pro and give every guest 100% at all times.

Tip 6

Training

Attention all employees. Regardless of the job, you should be well prepared and given all the tools and knowledge to do/be your best. This is especially true in the restaurant business, the ultimate service industry, A server may have previous experience and yet be new to an establishment. Training is a necessity. Most servers are impatient, as I was, and want to start earning the money right away. Service is service, but each restaurant has a different menu and policies. When you do your homework and familiarize yourself with the menu and restaurant policies, you will get off to a better start. Think like a professional. After all you are a professional.

Tip 7

Know the Restaurant

Guests ask a lot of questions. We all know this. Some will be in regard to the restaurant itself. For example: How long has the restaurant been open? What is the owner's name? What is the chef's name? What is the seating capacity? What are your hours of operation? Do you do banquets? Do you do catering? I could go on and on, but I think you get the point. You should be able to answer all restaurant-related questions asked. Your guests will know you're on the ball. Again, intelligence pays.

More Money!

More Money!!

Tip 8

Know the Surrounding Area

That's right—your guests are asking more questions. You will deal with a lot of guests that may be visiting from other areas. They may ask where a movie theater might be. Is there a nice jazz club close by? What about a challenging golf course? We want to go dancing, what do you suggest? If you can answer these simple questions, it will reflect greatly on you. Sound smart and be smart. Your guests appreciate the information and will usually leave a little more of that good ol' tip. Intelligence and information pay.

Tip 9

Know Your Menus
Both Food and Bar

Product knowledge is the backbone of all sales. Not only the food menu but the beverage menu as well. Obviously learn your menu thoroughly and familiarize yourself with the selection of beers both domestic and foreign. Learn your wine list, well liquors, call liquors, and house specialty drinks. Being able to answer these questions shows your guests you have a great knowledge of your job. A complete and thorough knowledge is essential to your success. Use mouth-watering descriptions whenever possible. Know the answers without hesitation at every table. Once again, knowledge pays.

Tip 10

Know Your Food Abbreviations

Some restaurants use a computer/POS system for placing orders. It is of the utmost importance that you know your codes, forwards and backwards, for each item on the menu. The reasons are obvious: you will not spend valuable time fumbling through code books looking up numbers. The flow of your fellow servers can be greatly affected by these delays. You would not want this to happen to you. Eliminate these stressful situations by knowing your codes.

Manual check writing still exists in some restaurants. In this case, you must know your abbreviations. Write clearly and be concise. Your chefs will appreciate this, and you will get the orders correctly. Avoid having to make an excuse to the guest for any delays due to a misread ticket in the kitchen. Remember, you are ultimately responsible for the table. Make things as easy as possible for all those concerned. Mistake-free shifts are awesome.

Tip 11

Write It Down

It seems impressive when a server remembers everything a party of six orders and manages to pull it off mistake-free. Imagine having a full section, twenty-five plus people. The possibility for error is huge. Don't take any chances. The times that impressed people the most, and I got the best tips, happened because I didn't make any mistakes. A guest is not going to care one way or the other whether you write it down or do it from memory. They just want it right. You, or anyone else who may deliver the food, won't have to ask anyone who gets what. This is also known as having to auction the food. Anyone knows exactly where it is going. This shows great coordination within the restaurant. Much more impressive than not writing it down and possibly making a mistake. Much more rewarding financially, as well.

Tip 12

Side Work

Side work is a variety of things that need to be completed before the restaurant opens. It is designed so the restaurant is ready to open and serve the public and the restaurant can have a nice flow to it. Things are ready to go. All successful sales people take time for preparation; your job should not be any different. Extra care with side work will help take care of the customers. Under normal conditions, side work is divided among the servers and bussers. If everyone completes their side work, the flow of the restaurant becomes much easier. When you need something, it's there. Eliminate delays! This is an area where staff members count on each other. Do your part and eliminate questions like who was supposed to cut lemons? Who didn't fill the ice buckets? Back up your crew. It is extremely important that you keep a good working relationship with your fellow crew members. Develop a reputation as someone who does their side work. The contrary could cost you not only work relationships, but tips and maybe even your job. Who needs the stress? Do your side work. After all you are a team player.

Tip 13

Table Numbers and Seat Positions

All restaurants have table numbers. All restaurants should have seat number/positions as well. On the rare occasion that the restaurant does not have specific seat positions, you should make up your own codes or nicely mention to your manager how this can help. The correct table number and seat position should be on all checks. This allows expediters, managers, or anyone to run food. No one should have to ask who gets what, if the information is correct. Auctioning is for amateurs. You are a PRO!!! Ladies first, clockwise around the table, and then the men. No cold food here!!! This shows great coordination within the restaurant.

Tip 14

Point Your Tables

The French have a saying: "Mise-en-place." This means "everything in its place." Before a guest is seated, it is the responsibility of the server to make sure the table is set correctly and completely. Guests stating they are short a water glass or bread plate indicates poor preparation and attention to their needs. Pointing your tables also means that you polish the silverware and glassware, make sure the salt and pepper shakers and sugar containers are full, and the chairs and surrounding area are clean. A first impression can go a long way. Be prepared. It's your job.

Tip 15

Teamwork

Teamwork starts with you. It is up to you to make sure your section is up to date and on schedule. If you rely on other servers to get you back on track, you may be in trouble. If they are busy themselves, you just may find yourself in the weeds. A nightmare for any server. I've been there before, and you don't want to go there. You may start to wonder why you are even in this business. The other side of teamwork is if you have the time to help, do so. Perhaps this means re-stocking a side station, watering other tables that are not in your section, running food, etc. Help each other get through the shift as smoothly as possible. Don't let your lack of help/teamwork come back to haunt you. Be a team player.

Tip 16

Side Stations

It is of the utmost importance that you maintain your side stations. These are provided for the convenience of the servers and bussers. Imagine having to go back to the kitchen for every little thing you needed. If you take the last of something, please replace it. This is a team-oriented environment. We must all help each other. We all know how great it is when the things you need are there. When they are not, it can get pretty annoying. Be considerate of others and think of everyone, not just yourself. This helps with the flow of the restaurant and, once again, eliminates unnecessary stress. This applies to the bussers as well.

Tip 17

Communication

Communication with the kitchen and other servers is very important. If one of the specials has been 86'd and you sold one to your guests, it can be very embarrassing. It can result in disappointment on their part, since they were looking forward to the promised item. On top of that, they have to look through the menu again. This could annoy a customer. At this point, a sincere "I am very sorry" wouldn't hurt, along with some alternative suggestions within the same price range.

The term 86'd is used to indicate that you have run out of an item or it is no longer available. It can also mean an establishment is through with you and is asking you to leave. In other words, you are getting thrown out.

A little trivia: The term 86'd has its roots in England. Traditionally the alcohol/liquor served in an English pub was 151 proof or higher. When a customer seemed to be getting a little too drunk, or out of hand, the bartender, from this point on, would serve the customer only 86 proof alcohol. Hence, he/she had been 86'd.

Tip 18

No Accidents

Let each other know what's happening in the restaurant. If you are approaching someone from behind, say, behind you. If you are about to pass someone, perhaps a little tap on the shoulder to let them know you are there. If coming around a corner, say "corner." Avoid collisions. Go in the In door and out the Out door. Other forms of communication are between you and your support staff. If you are asking someone to get you something you need for a table, make sure they hear you and acknowledge you. Guests should very rarely/or never have to ask for anything. See Tip 35. If a guest is forced to ask more than once, it is a reflection on your service, even if you asked someone else to get it and they forgot it. Remember you are ultimately responsible for your tables. Stay focused, be aware of what's happening, and communicate with each other.

Tip 19

Acknowledge Your Guests

Acknowledging your guests is very important in setting an early tone for the table. An ignored guest can become rude, upset, and a little more demanding than was necessary. Start out with happy guests. If you are busy, "Hello, I will be with you in a moment" can buy you the time you need. The guest has been acknowledged and will usually understand. Most restaurants have a policy in place where you are required to, at least, make an acknowledgement within two minutes after the guests have been seated.

Another point of importance is not to ignore/neglect anyone at the table. If you have a party of six, pay some attention to all of your guests.

Acknowledge, at some point, everyone. Don't make anyone feel invisible. It's not a good feeling. Potentially a tough spot to get out of especially if that particular person ends up paying the tab/bill. Engage the whole table.

Tip 20

Reading the Customer

At this point, introducing yourself and welcoming the guests to the restaurant is very important. You are in a position to make your guests feel very special. Inform the guests who you are and that you would personally like to welcome them to (name of your restaurant). "It will be my pleasure to take care of you this evening." This is very powerful. This will put smiles on the faces of your guests and start the evening on a positive note.

You should vary your approach to every table. A canned presentation can bore guests. Be relaxed and confident, otherwise a guest may get the sense you just want to get it over with. Being stiff or rehearsed gives the impression the server is bored, lazy, or doesn't care — the exact opposite of individualized personal service. The excellent servers will treat every table like it's the only one in their section. Two elderly couples need a different type of approach/service than two high school kids on a prom date. Get a sense of what they want and customize your service.

Tip 21

The Single Diner

Do not forget about the single diner. Be careful what you say or how you act. Certain phrases or comments can make one feel uncomfortable, for example, guys using pick up lines. A good place to seat a single diner may be a booth or against a wall. A poor place may be a table in the middle of the room. Perhaps they are on a business trip or just out for a nice quite meal. No matter what the case, show respect, make them feel comfortable, and provide great service as usual. Do not forget, the single diner also tips.

Tip 22

Never Assume

How many times have we assumed something that turns out to be the complete opposite? In the restaurant business you will deal with a variety of characters. Pre-judge no one. You never know whom you are dealing with. That tattered looking man in the corner might be the local newspaper's restaurant critic. Who knows? Treat every guest like a V.I.P. Everyone deserves the best possible service you can provide. 100% of the time. There just may be a big surprise in it for you. Don't take any chances.

Tip 23

V.I.P.s

Very important persons. Once in a while your manager/boss/owner will say "This is a V.I.P. table, and I want you to give it extra special service." Every guest you serve should be treated like a V.I.P. They are all important to you. Your guests, whoever they might be, are the ones paying your bills. Give them all equal respect and great service. Everyone deserves it.

If you have the ability to turn it up a notch, for a so-called V.I.P., then you are not doing your best for the rest of your customers.

Everyone deserves you at your best!

Tip 24

Check Averages

You will win some, and you will win some big. Stay positive and upbeat regardless of the tip. Remember, some tips will be better than average. Stay positive and keep a good attitude. It will all equal out in the end. You don't get rich or go broke off of one table. The goal is to get the most out of each table. And get this, you will never know if you did or didn't. It is what it is.

Some servers after receiving a so called bad tip (remember you still won) return to the floor with a slightly different attitude. "Man, what a lousy tip. Those cheap #*^&%$^$ people. I can't believe it. I gave them great service." Perhaps they are in that five percent bracket we discussed earlier. Let it go immediately. Your current and future guests had nothing to do with it. Again, stay positive and maintain that positive attitude.

Something to think about. If a guest leaves you a well above average tip, which we all love, would you feel obligated to return some of it. Probably not. Remember, any tip is a win for you.

Tip 25

Dealing with Children

There is something about children we must remember. They are people, too. Most servers see children come into the restaurant and think "Oh Lord, please don't put them in my section. What, I get the kiddie section tonight?"

You can turn this to your advantage. Just involve them. It's that simple. The parents notice these things and appreciate it very much. One, you relieve some of the stress of the parents having to pay attention to the children at all times, and two, the children are having a much better time and are less difficult. Have fun with the children. The parents will notice your efforts and say thank you with a generous tip. It works. Besides, we all have a little kid inside us just waiting to come out and play. Now's your chance.

Tip 26

Working with the Kitchen

Working successfully with the kitchen requires good communication, as well as, complete, concise, and correct orders. Butting heads with the chefs causes problems for both parties. If a restaurant uses abbreviations, make sure that you know all of them and use them at all times. Be sure and write clearly and legibly. Some chefs will actually give a ticket back to the server and say write/input the correct abbreviations/codes. This does nothing but delay the entire process, and delays can do nothing but hurt you and potentially upset the guest. Most restaurants use computer/POS systems for placing orders. Make sure you order the correct items. Always double check to be 100% sure. Always.

Tip 27

Working with the Bar

When ordering your drinks, make sure you write clearly and use the correct abbreviations. If the bartender can read your tickets, your drinks will be delivered in a more timely fashion. Once again, most restaurants use a computer/POS system for ordering. Make sure you input the correct drinks/wine and double check to make sure. No mistakes. A lot of servers approach the bartender and start verbally ordering drinks. It's on the ticket already, and he/she has a lot on their mind and do not need to be confused. Wait your turn. Your drinks are coming.

When getting change for a customer, make sure the bartender gives you your change broken down to make it easier for the customer to give you your tip. Guests having to ask for change again may find it an inconvenience and tip you less than they would have otherwise. Make it easy.

Tip 28

Your Own Restaurant

Most people wish they could own their own business and be their own boss. Accept the fact that you are an independent contractor/salesperson who has total control over your own income. Suggestive selling isn't forcing guests to buy anything; it is simply a way to enhance the dining experience and make them feel more comfortable and welcome. Guests will, more often than not, tip more when they have been pleasantly guided though their dining experience.

There are a lot of headaches and responsibilities that go along with ownership. If you think about it, as a server, this is the perfect situation for you. You have been given a number of tables in a section of the restaurant for the evening. These tables are your responsibility. In your mind this section should be treated as if it were your own restaurant. You are provided with all the materials you need to be successful at zero cost to you. Sweet. All the overhead is paid for by someone else. Sweet. Do your best and give it your all as if it was your own place. Passion is the key!

Tip 29

Table Maintenance

Table maintenance is extremely important. During the course of the evening there will be several courses served, especially with you up-selling appetizers and desserts with such vigor. This will require new silverware, plates, and the like. Replace items before needed so the guest doesn't have to ask. Not good service. You, the server, know what's coming, so be prepared. Pay attention and stay focused. Table maintenance also includes the removal of any unnecessary items such as silverware no longer needed, dirty/finished plates, or glass ware.

Tip 30

Section Awareness

The smooth flow of an evening has a lot to do with being aware — at all times — of exactly where every table is in the service process. Walking through the restaurant with the proverbial blinders on inhibits your ability to be aware of your guest's needs. Every time you walk through your section you should be scanning all your tables to see what is needed or if a guest may be trying to get your attention. Remember, anticipating a guest's needs can leave a favorable impression. If a guest has to ask for something, perhaps more water, bread, etc., you are not paying attention. This could have an impact on your tip. Pay attention! Give your guest plenty of reasons to tip to the fullest.

Tip 31

Wine Service

Whoever orders the bottle of wine, for the table, is the host/ess of that bottle. Be it a man or a woman. This is the person you present the bottle to for initial taste and approval. When approved, you serve the ladies first, moving clockwise around the table, then the men, and last the host/ess. Only fill the wine glass half to two-thirds full. Keep an eye on the wine glass levels. It's your responsibility to be pouring the wine for your guests, unless otherwise notified. If your guests have to pour the wine for themselves, it shows a lack of attention on your part. You want people to enjoy, and appreciate, your attention and excellent service. However, on rare occasions some guests prefer to pour their own. No problem.

Tip 32

The Art of Listening
Special Request Orders

You must master the art of listening. Simply learn when to — how can I put this politely — shut up. Servers must listen to not only what the customers are saying, servers must also listen to what they are not saying. Reading between the lines in some cases. Are they in a hurry? Do they want to take their time? Is it a special celebration? Etc. Pay attention!!! If they are having a difficult time making up their mind, be prepared to make suggestions.

Some special requests happen simply because some people like to mix and match or order something that is not on the menu. Most restaurants will honor these requests if possible. However, some requests are for health reasons. Some people are allergic to nuts, for example, and can become very ill or even die. Perhaps extreme, but possible. Not all ingredients are visible. Pay attention to these special requests. Think about this. What would you do, or how would you feel, if you had a sick person on your hands? Get the order right. Some people are vegetarians and ask for special items. Make sure you know the ingredients in every dish the restaurant offers. Once again be prepared to make suggestions. People really appreciate your knowledge and guidance.

Tip 33

Timing of Courses

There is no need to rush anyone though dinner, and there is certainly no reason to keep them waiting. For one thing you need to develop a feel for what the timing in the kitchen is like. Early in the evening, food service/preparation will be a lot faster than during the rush or busy times. Also chefs work at different speeds. Know who is behind the line during your shift. This will assist you in knowing when to fire orders. Knowing the timing involved helps avoid doing things like serving the entrée before they're finished with their salads or serving their entrées about the time they were expecting desserts.

Tip 34

Food Presentation
and Serving of the Entrées, etc.

Visually appealing food just tastes better. Before you serve your orders make sure the plate is clean around the edges. Make sure you add the proper garnishes (i.e., lemon with fish, parsley, etc.) and by all means make sure the order is correct. When delivering the entrées to the table, serve the ladies first and announce the entrées as you serve. Adds a nice personal touch. When serving, serve plates from the right with your right hand and when clearing/removing, remove from the left with your left hand. You do not want to put your arm or armpit in someone's face. Place the main part of the entrée, for example the steak, at the six o'clock position directly in front of the guest. You want the plate to be placed conveniently for the guests. Remember the plate is usually hot, so be sure to let them know. If improperly placed, the guest will usually move the plate and if it is hot could burn themselves. When everyone has been served, make sure you say something like "Enjoy your dinners. Does everyone here have everything they need?" Great! If everyone is happy, check back within two minutes to make sure the food has been properly prepared and they are still happy.

Tip 35

Anticipation

One definition of anticipate is "to foresee a request and perform in advance." Anticipating a guest's needs, and performing them before they ask, will impress. For example, when your guests are close to running out of butter, low on water, getting low on bread, etc., and you take care of these issues before they have to ask, once again, it will impress. Anticipating guest's needs before they ask is the mark of a true professional. It shows that you are paying attention, and believe me, it is noticed. It can only help lead to a nice big tip.

Tip 36

Memory

Memory plays a key role. When guests ask for something, they generally need the requested item right away. Remember it and do it. Don't wait. You may forget. This is not good. Do not stop at another table and take an order or chit chat. When a guest asks for something, this is the first thing you should do and then move on. Forget to forget or simply remember to remember. It will make the difference between customers enjoying their meals to the fullest or wondering what happened to the requested item. Concentrate and stay focused.

Tip 37

Tipping Your Help

Your support help can be the difference between having a smooth shift or a stressful one. The busser's job is designed to do specific things for you and the restaurant, and they work for a percentage of the tips you make that evening. Whether you get excellent support or lousy support from your bussers, your overall tip can be affected. Regardless of the support, you must always remember the server is ultimately responsible for the table. Doesn't matter where the breakdown may occur, it's on you. Please be generous and tip accordingly. At least what you are required to tip. This goes for the bartenders as well. Don't forget him/her. They help you too. With great help, perhaps a little more. The bussers/bartenders know when they are not being treated fairly. Trust me. If you have a poor tipping reputation, the bussers/bartenders may not be there for you when you need them the most. Servers generally complain about not getting enough help, but if you really look at the overall picture, bussers do a tremendous amount of work for you. Tipping your support staff fairly is the right thing to do.

Treat your support staff with respect and an occasional "Thank you for your help, you did a great job tonight." This will be much appreciated. After all, they are doing most of the dirty work. We are all on the same team.

If It's Not Fun,

You Will Not Be That Successful

Tip 38

Goals, Incentives, and Promos

It is important to set a goal for the evening and have some incentives. Realistic goals, of course. Your goals can be the number of bottles of wine you sell, the number of specials you sell, or any number of things. Setting goals will give you more drive and desire to meet them. More sales, the bigger the bottom line, the more tips in your pocket. Having an incentive is huge motivation. It's human nature. Have your manager set some goals for the evening, perhaps a contest of some kind, and watch the sales soar.

Money!

Money!!

Money!!!

What is a goal?

A dream with a deadline!

What Kinds Of Goals Do I Need?

Result goals: The end result I'm striving for.

Action goals: The things I need to do to get the results.

Two key words:

Realistic and *Achievable*.

Who sets goals?

The most successful people!

Facts about setting goals:

• 84 percent of people have no goals at all.

• 13 percent of people kinda/sorta have goals, but don't follow the rules.

• 3 percent of people set goals the right way and earn a substantial amount more money than non-goal setters. A fact!!

• 94 percent of written goals are achieved.

Areas to focus on:

Attitude

Skills

Habits

Tip 39

Up-selling – Give Yourself a Raise

There is a saying in the restaurant business: "If you want a raise, you don't go to your boss, you go to the menu." By selling an appetizer, a dessert or two, call liquor versus well liquor, etc., your bottom line increases as well as your tip. You will be amazed at the difference this will make over time. Take a look at the charts ahead. It may be only a dollar or two at a time, but it adds up quickly.

The following tip

comparison charts

will be an eye opener

Enjoy all

That Extra Money!!!

Tip Comparison Chart

David

Average Check total (two persons) $ 38.00

2 desserts (Suggestive Selling) $ 7.00

2 glasses of wine $ 7.00

Total check $ 52.00

15% Tip $ 7.80

Tips/Shift $ 78.00

Tips/week 5 shifts/Week $390.00

Tips/Year (50 weeks) $ 19,500.00

Michael

Average Check total (two persons) $ 38.00

2 desserts (Suggestive Selling) $ 0

2 Glasses of Wine $ 0

Total Check $ 38.00

15% Tip $ 5.70

Tips/Shift $ 57.00

Tips/Week (5 shifts/week) $ 285.00

Tips/Year (50 Weeks) $ 14,250.00

The difference: $ 14.00 in total check

$ 2.10 in the 15% tip

$ 21.00 for the overall night

$ 105.00 for the week

For the Year

$5250.00

Proof Sheet

Check Total Average x Number Of People = Sales

$15.00 x 20 per day = $300.00 Sales

$17.00 x 20 per day = $340.00 Sales

INCREASE = $40.00 x 20 days = $800.00 Sales

x 12 MONTHS = $9600.00 PER YEAR

IN GROSS SALES

Server Tip Increase From 15% To 17%

$136.00 Per Month

Or

$1632.00 Per Year

*These numbers are hypothetical, on this and the previous page, for the sake of showing you the potential of up-selling. Averages for your restaurant may vary.

A roast Is done,

A guest Is Finished!

Bonus Section

Some suggestions in up-selling

Up-selling or suggestive selling is the best way to increase the check's bottom line. The bigger the bottom, line the bigger the tip. The following is a set of very powerful suggestions that will make this happen. I have utilized these phrases/techniques consistently, with great success. You will be pleasantly surprised how effective these little anecdotes will work for you. Let's touch on the four major courses your guests will experience during the evening.

- Beverage service
- Appetizers
- Main course
- Desserts

Make yourself more Money

Beverage Service

After your approach to the table, with that infectious smile, that great attitude, and of course individualized personalized service, you will start their evening with an offer to get them a beverage. If you have a wine list, present it at this time. "May I start you out with a cocktail this evening, or perhaps you would like to look over our wine list. We have a wonderful selection to choose from. If you have any questions or would like some recommendations please feel free to ask." Now for some of those suggestions I promised. Used consistently they will generate larger sales making you, your support staff, and the restaurant a lot more money.

A guest orders a vodka tonic. What do you do? Are you an order taker or an order maker? Here is where product knowledge is essential. A great opportunity to up-sell has just presented itself. Don't miss it. Would you prefer Absolute, Stoli, Grey Goose, and so forth. Always offer an up-sell on any of the well liquors. Run, Gin, Scotch, etc. Most guests will select one of your suggestions. Others may not be aware that there is such a variety of selections and may try something, other than the usual. Give them all an opportunity. To the best of my knowledge most well drinks are around $4.50-$5.50. Call liquors may be somewhere between $6.00-$10.00. Depends on the restaurant, of course.

Makes a huge difference on the check. I find this next suggestion to be very important. For example the guest is having a Beefeaters gin and tonic. When asking a guest if they would like another drink do not use the word another. Be specific and specify the drink by name. "Can I get you a Beefeaters and tonic?" If they are having a Budweiser "Can I get you a Budweiser?" Eliminate the word another from your vocabulary. This will help in your sales. The word another can/may indicate they have had enough.

Let's not forget the children. Just the mention of a Shirley Temple, non-alcoholic strawberry daiquiris, or fruit drinks will add to the check. Perhaps a double Similac on the rocks for the little one/baby. One of my favorites. A little humor never hurts and besides the parents love it. Hmm, the bottom line seems to be getting bigger. But wait there's more.

This is a sure-fire way to improve your wine sales by the bottle versus the glass. This can also have a huge impact on the bottom line and is surprisingly easy to do. All you have to do is ask. Don't be afraid to ask. The key here is to listen to what they are saying. Some guests will always order a bottle of wine while others, in this case, the majority of your guests will say something like "I think we will start out with two glasses of chardonnay." The key here is the word start. The word start means that they will probably have more later. Usually with the entrée. This is your golden opportunity to sell a bottle.

This proven response is extremely effective. "Perhaps you will allow me to bring a bottle of chardonnay for the table. This way there is no delay in waiting for your next glass, as well as, making it readily available for your convenience." A good percentage of your guests will say "Good idea, bring us a bottle." Be an order maker not an order taker. This way you only make one trip instead or two. Some may indicate that they can't finish a whole bottle. Inform them they can cork the bottle and finish their wine later at their own convenience. It works.

> *The laws regarding being able to take an unfinished bottle of wine home may vary from state to state. Make sure you know the law.

However, some will order different types of wine, perhaps one glass of red and one glass of white. A little tougher scenario to sell each a bottle so don't forget to offer more later.

Here are some very good reasons, for you personally, to get that bottle on the table. It can save you valuable time at a time when you can least afford it. You may be extremely busy. You could be behind seven tickets at the bar, and by the time you deliver the wine, your guests may be nearly finished with their dinners. Or even worse, they could be finished. At this point, they may not want it anymore. It's happened. Trust me. Not good. Not only is having a bottle at the table convenient for the guest but maybe even more so for yourself. Hmm, the bottom line keeps getting bigger and bigger. Good job! Any plans for that extra money you are making?

What is the best way to become good at anything you do?

Practice!

Practice!

Practice!

Appetizers/Starters

Appetizers or starters are a great way to add to the bottom line. Some guests will always order an appetizer while others never do. This is where the 90% rule can apply. (Refer to tip #5) Time to sell. Saying the standard — would you like to try/start out with an appetizer this evening — gives the guest an easy out. No thank you was the answer I got more often than not. Now what? What can I do or say to be more successful in this area? An experiment I tried, myself, yielded remarkable results. For one week I approached my guests with "Would you like to try/start out with an appetizer this evening?" Three out of ten tables ordered an appetizer. Three out of ten in baseball makes you a superstar, but it is not good enough in the restaurant business, or any other sales job.

The following week I used a different approach/ speech. "In regard to our appetizers, you should experience the calamari or bruschetta. It's a great way to start the evening and, as a rule, there is enough for two or more." Any guests who may not have intended to order an appetizer now simply because you made it sound more fun and exciting. My appetizer sales climbed to seven out of ten. My sales more than doubled, and even the chef wondered what the heck was going on. I am a graduate of Bennett/Stellar university which, among other curriculum, teaches language skills and the power of language/persuasive techniques. Lawyers use these techniques all the time. After all their job is to persuade people. I shared this information with the staff, and sales increased across the board.

Choose any or all of the appetizers from your own menu, change your approach from the standard speech to a more exciting presentation and see the difference. Very important to eliminate the word try. You will be surprised by the results. I promise you. Bigger the bottom line will result in bigger tips.

Entrées

Time for the main course. In addition to the menu's entrée selections there are usually a number of entrée specials to offer your guests. Usually the specials are higher-priced selections, which gives you an opportunity to increase the bottom line. It is extremely important to offer the specials to every table. If for some reason you decide not to offer the specials to a table because you are too busy and don't have the time, remember, you probably presented the specials to a neighboring table, and by not presenting the specials to your new guests, they will feel slighted. In most cases the slighted guests may ask if there are any specials, knowing full well there are, and you may find yourself in an uncomfortable situation. People pay attention and generally know what's going on around them. Don't short-change anyone. Be the professional you are and give everyone your best V.I.P. treatment. Don't take any chances. It's not worth it.

When presenting the specials to your guests make them sound like exactly what they are, special. Use mouth-watering descriptions and describe, in detail, the preparation, the sauces, the accompanying items, and of course how terrific they are. Remember those language skills. A lot of people will trust your judgment and order one. Specials are a good ones to use for the goals you set for the evening.

In some cases a guest is going to ask you what your favorite entrée is on the menu. When answering your guest, don't forget to reaffirm how terrific the specials are along with some of your personal favorites. When a guest asks if a particular item is good, never answer with anything negative even if you personally don't care for it. Your guest, after all, may like it. You don't want to project anything negative. Always be positive.

Desserts

Presenting/offering desserts can be a lot of fun and a great way to add to the bottom line. Your guests have finished their entrees, the table has been properly cleared and it is now time to present desserts. This is a great opportunity to have some fun. It's your final chance to continue building rapport and perhaps inject a little humor. If you can get your guests to finish the evening with a little laugh, you most likely just made yourself a little more money. Showtime.

Once again using mouth-watering phrases and detailed descriptions of the available dessert selections, your guests will not be able to resist. Quite often you will get the response "I'm so full I just couldn't have another bite, even though they sound so good." This next tip is an extremely successful up-selling technique that will, not only add a little humor to the situation, but double or even triple your dessert sales.

You have a table of four. You have just done your dessert presentation and the table says no thank you, with the usual afore mentioned response. At this point you might say something like "You know, today is your lucky day." The guest will always say "Oh, why is that?" "Because each one of our desserts comes with four forks." Not only does this get a laugh but now they start to think maybe they can share a dessert and each have a bite or two. The seed has been planted. More often than not the table will get at least one dessert to share. This works so well you will use it the rest of your restaurant career.

Don't forget to offer coffees. When you do sell desserts, coffee usually follows. Perhaps an espresso or cappuccino. Another potential sale would be coffee drinks. Baileys and coffee, Irish coffee, Kahlua and coffee, just to name a few, are very popular after dinner drinks. Cognacs, Grand Marnier, etc., is another possibility. If the restaurant has a list of these selections, always present it. All of the above is a great way to increase the bottom line. More money!!!

All you have to do

is ask!!

Occasionally Complaints Will Happen

You approach the table at about the two-minute mark, after serving the entrees, and ask if the dinners have been prepared properly and is everyone happy. Make sure you specify or individualize the meals when asking. For example. "Has your filet been cooked to your liking sir/mam?"

The guest may respond with "My food is cold, and I ordered my steak medium rare, and this is well done."

Hmm,

What do you do?

Tip 40

Difficult Guest Problem Solving

We all dread the difficult guests or crabby customers. It does not have to be a difficult and stressful experience. There are six easy steps to solve these problems.

1. Listen: The answer is usually within the complaint.

2. Empathize: Show that you genuinely care.

3. Clarify: Be clear on exactly what the problem is.

4. Repeat: Repeat to the customer the problem so there is no doubt what the problem is.

5. Apologize: A genuine apology can soothe a difficult customer.

6. Resolve: You have a clear idea of the problem. Take action to solve the problem.

This series of steps will help to defuse the difficult/complaining customer. Complaints should never be taken personally or allowed to ruin the rest of your evening. Occasionally, it just comes with the territory. Check with your manager for help in solving issues you are having difficulty with. Leave no loose ends.

Is the customer always right? Well, no... not exactly. However, we always have to let the guest win. They have to believe they are right.

This is a perfect opportunity,

in an odd sort of way,

to create a lifetime customer.

Tip 41

Check Delivery

When the server approaches the table with the check in hand before offering coffee or desserts, and says "Will that be all?" it may give the impression that you are through with the table. This is perhaps the biggest complaint you will never hear from your guests. Never offer or present the check before your guest is absolutely finished for the evening. They could potentially want something else like coffee, desserts, after dinner drinks, etc. If they see the check in hand, they just might feel uneasy or consider it inconvenient at this point and simply say they don't want anything else, even though they may have wanted something. You will never know, now. You most likely have cost yourself an opportunity for a sale and a bigger bottom line. Translation: Bigger tip. Don't be lazy or shortcut your service to any of your guests. Don't leave any money on the table!!

Have you ever presented or dropped off a check before asking if your guests were finished? You assumed they were, or perhaps hoped they were. Lo and behold they want a dessert and coffee. The best of the best, the pros, would never do this. You should feel a little embarrassed at this point. You stopped short of finishing your job, and the customer called it on you. Not only that but now you have to rewrite or reprint the check, which may turn out to be an inconvenience for you. There is some good news. The check's bottom line just increased, in spite of yourself, and hopefully made more money. Sell all the way to the end.

One more thing. Always deliver the check yourself. Do not have the busser or anyone else do this for you. This is your last chance to thank your guests and show that you cared. Be in control all the way until the end. It pays!

Tip 42

Special Occasions

Keep an eye out for any of your guests who may be celebrating something special. Perhaps a birthday, anniversary, promotions, etc. A little extra touch and that special attention goes a long way. Usually someone will inform the restaurant while making a reservation about the special occasion. Or, one of the guests will inform you, the server. Your establishment usually has a policy in place for these occasions. Perhaps a complementary dessert, drink, or appetizer. Don't forget. Individualized personal attention makes each of us feel special. After all it is their special night, and you have the power to make it exactly that, special.

One Final Story For You...

I consider this, perhaps, the best advice anyone has ever given me during my career as a server.

I was about six months into my restaurant career as a server. One particular evening I was out of control, running around like a mad man, in the weeds, buried, you name it, that was me. The thought of quitting had entered my mind. What am I doing? Who needs this? A fellow server named Doug, a real pro, took me to the side and asked me to settle down and take a break for a few minutes. He said he wanted to share something with me. I looked at him like he was crazy. Now, I said. Are you nuts? I have at least twenty things to do. I can't stop now. He insisted and I reluctantly gave in. It was the best two-minute break I ever took.

He had noticed that I was losing it and out of control. He asked me how many things I had to do to catch up. I said at least twenty. Why? His said to me that I still had twenty, or so, things to do no matter what, right? Now I could do these things out of control or under control, the choice was mine. After some thought I realized that under control was much more appealing and made tremendous sense. With this new-found mind set everything became a lot less stressful, and the guests never knew if I was stressed or not, and I became a better server immediately. It was great advice. From that point on a guest would occasionally comment on how easy I made the job look and that I must have been in the business a long time. I simply said thank you for noticing and I appreciated it very much. It felt really good to be recognized for my efforts.

Be in control.

It's the obvious choice.

Tip 43

Show That You Care/Be Sincere

Showing that you genuinely care about the people sitting in your section is extremely important to the guest's overall experience. Be sincere in your actions. You must care that your guests have the best food and get the best value. You must care that your guests receive the best service and have a memorable evening and the best time they can possibly have. When guests recognize, and they will, that you care about their dining experience, they will usually show their appreciation in two ways. First, a sincere thank you for a wonderful evening. Second, just might be a more generous tip. Both of these scenarios, together, would be ideal. Not only should you feel good about the great job you just did, but you continue to keep giving yourself a raise. This is so exciting. All that extra money. Keep it up.

Caring and sincerity

are the Key!

Tip 44

Professional Responses

When a guest asks for something like some more water, for example, you should be polite and sound literate and professional with your response.

  • Good — "Certainly, I will be happy to get that for you."

  •Not good — "You bet, pal. I'll grab that for you."

  • Good — "Absolutely, I'll be right back with some water."

  • Not good — "You got it, back in a few."

  • Good — "I'll get you some water right away sir/mam."

  • Not good — "Sure thing, buddy. Just give me a minute."

I think you get the idea. Be courteous and polite and most of all be professional.

One thing to consider is that about ninety-nine percent of your guests are not your immediate friends or acquaintances. This is a professional atmosphere, your place of work. Treat them professionally, with respect, and don't assume you can get away with

certain verbal liberties. They should not be ad-
dressed as buddies or dudes. You don't know these
people, and you are certainly not a guest of the table. You are in a domestic capacity. Don't linger.
Stealth service is what I call it. In and out and hard-
ly noticed.

The real secret of success

is enthusiasm

Things to Practice

Here are some important points to remember while on the job. The best are always working to improve their skill levels. It will pay off. I promise.

- Do your best, be the best.

- Polish your job skills.

- Practice people/listening (rapport) skills.

- Learn communication skills.

- Know hospitality industry terms.

- Practice stress elimination skills.

- Know everything there is to know about your restaurant.

- Work on retention and memory skills.

Tip 45

Return/Regular Customers

It is of the utmost importance that the service you provide is a huge reason why people want to return to your restaurant. The more a customer returns, and perhaps requests you over and over again, usually means more money for you. People request certain servers because they like and trust them. This is very comforting to the guest, and they feel that the service experience will be consistently great. Don't let them down. People have very short memories. The great part about this is return/request customers have a tendency to be a little more generous. This, I can definitely speak from experience.

Another thing about the return/regular customer is, simply put, they like the restaurant and you. They are impressed when you remember things like what drink they usually order or their names. Practice these retention and memory skills and pay attention. You never know when you will see these people again. Hopefully sooner than later. You are the restaurant's most important and best form of advertising. Do your best and represent well.

A good waiter
can save a bad meal,
but a good meal
can't save a bad waiter

Summary

Apply these techniques faithfully and you will see an increase in the bottom line and your gratuities. Guaranteed!! After you spend some time practicing and remembering these topics, you will also begin to see a noticeable improvement in your service abilities. You will begin to notice a better flow to your job. You will become less stressed and more comfortable with your customers and be able to handle larger sections. Once again, this can only mean more tips. More money. As I mentioned earlier in the book, these are the things the best of the best do on a regular basis.

I myself utilized these techniques for years. My check averages per person/table were consistently higher and the tips, overall, averaged at least twenty percent and more. What jobs do you know of that consistently pay an average of twenty to forty dollars an hour? Not many. Now get out there and be your best. Good luck!!!

Tip$ For Better Tip$—

Menu For Success

Attention food and beverage industry!

For more information on the availability of *Tips For Better Tips — Menu For Success,* you can contact me via e-mail: capelotodavid@yahoo.com or phone: 480-272-0740. All questions welcome. Also, now available on Amazon/Kindle books. Your staff will appreciate this knowledge and let's not forget this is a Win-Win situation for all. A small investment in yourself, with a big payoff.

About the Author

David S. Capeloto has assembled the ultimate guide that every server in the food and beverage industry should read. David's twenty-five years as a professional, on many levels in the industry, has given him invaluable incite, as well as hands-on experience. David's resume also includes management positions, two cruise ships, the Four Seasons Resort Hotel (Wailea property on Maui), the Lahaina Yacht Club, the Royal Palms Resort (as captain of banquets) in Scottsdale, Arizona, and more.

David is also a graduate of Bennett/Stellar University in the field of Neuro-Linguistic Programming, NLP. He also earned diplomas in the field of Hypnotherapy, Reiki (levels 1&2), and is a certified health and success coach.

David is also a musician and artist. David has played professional jazz/blues/cocktail piano for years, has given piano lessons, and sold some of his works of art.

David currently resides in Mesa, Arizona.

Good luck to everyone!

Have some fun!